# About this Book

What was it like to grow up in the 1950s? The Second World War had ended five years earlier, but its aftermath lingered on well into the next decade. There were still shortages of food and other essential commodities. The War had destroyed many homes and the housing shortage was desperate.

Gradually as the decade progressed, conditions began to improve. It was a time of excitement and change. Everyone hoped that the coronation of Queen Elizabeth II in 1953, would usher in a new 'Elizabethan era'.

The world was changing fast – there were new inventions and the beginning of the space age. But it was a turbulent world. Over all the 1950s hung the worry of the atom bomb, and around the world the new-found peace did not last long. There were wars, revolutions and refugees.

In this book Jeremy Pascall has vividly described these exciting times and tells us what it was like to live in this decade of rapid change and many challenges.

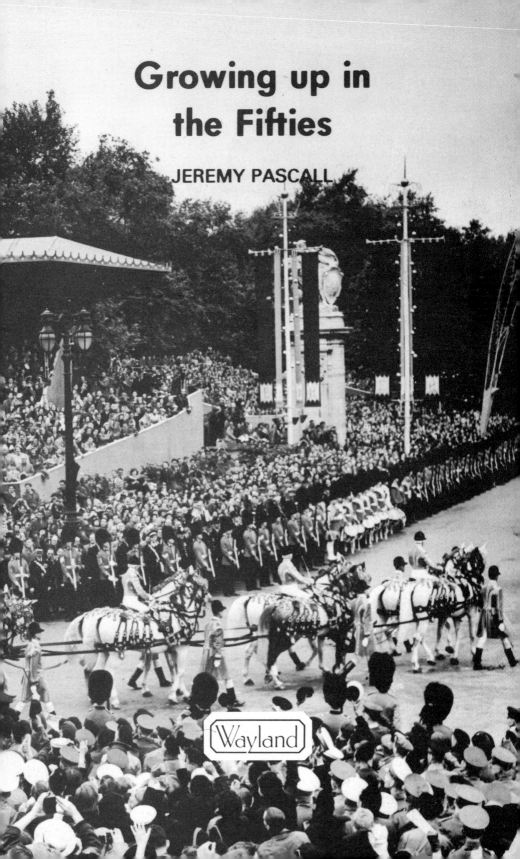

# Growing up in
# the Fifties

## JEREMY PASCALL

Wayland

# Growing up in Other Times

**Frontispiece:** The golden state coach carries the Queen through cheering London crowds, to her coronation

ISBN 0 85340 754 1

Copyright © 1980 by Wayland (Publishers) Ltd

First published in 1980 by Wayland (Publishers) Ltd,
49 Lansdowne Place, Hove, East Sussex, BN3 1HF, England

Second impression 1982
Third impression 1983

Text set in 12 pt. VIP Univers by Trident Graphics Limited,
Reigate, Surrey
Printed and bound in Great Britain at The Pitman Press, Bath

# Contents

# 1  Life at Home

The boys and girls who grew up in the years between 1950 and 1959 lived in times that were often difficult, sometimes dangerous and frequently exciting. The Second World War had not long ended and there were still many shortages of food and other essential goods. But there was a lot to look forward to now that the world was at peace again. Life could only get better and the conditions in which people lived, worked, went to school and enjoyed themselves could only improve.

In 1951 the Festival of Britain was held in London to celebrate the beginning of a prosperous and enterprising future, and two years later another great celebration was held for the coronation of Queen Elizabeth II.

For children in that decade the years brought the new excitements of television and rock 'n' roll; there were new heroes doing adventurous things like climbing the world's highest mountain or running the mile in less than four minutes. As the years passed there was more money to spend; many families had cars and could go away for holidays – undreamed of luxuries a few years earlier. Children again had comics and sweets and plenty to eat.

**After the War** During the War which lasted from 1939 to 1945, large areas of British cities were destroyed by German bombs. Whole streets of houses were flattened, making thousands of people homeless. The ugly scars which were left became 'adventure playgrounds' for children. One of the most important tasks which now faced the country was to build new homes, schools and factories, to replace those lost in the War.

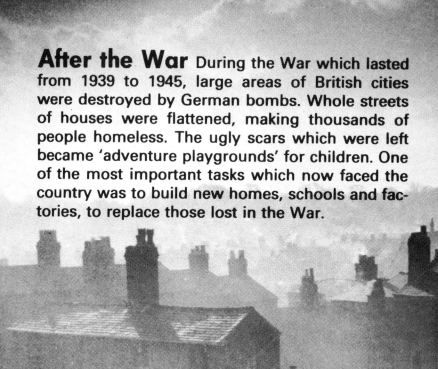

**Rationing** During the War food was so short that it had to be carefully shared out and everyone was given a ration book with tokens inside. By giving a token to the shopkeeper, people were allowed their small amounts of food. Things were not much better in the Fifties. Butter, cheese, bacon, meat, tea and sugar were still rationed up until 1954. The housewife in the picture is tearing up her ration book, after years of short supplies.

## The need for new homes

Some people still lived in old, unsafe and insanitary houses because the War had prevented new, modern ones being built. Many people had no baths or hot running water and toilets were often outside the house. Many children grew up in dirty, unsuitable and even dangerous homes. As soon as the War ended it was seen that such conditions had to be improved. Houses with proper bathrooms and toilets and, if possible, gardens, had to be built and the wealth of the country and its people had to be increased. A great effort was made to pull down slums like these.

**'Pre-fabs'** Too many people needed new houses. They could not be built quickly enough. As a temporary measure 'pre-fabs' (short for pre-fabricated) houses were built. These were just boxes made of asbestos sheets that could be quickly and easily erected on bomb sites and other cleared land. They were only intended to last for a few years until real houses, made of brick, could be built. In fact, thousands of people are still living in them today.

**Sweet rationing** Sweets were luxuries in the Fifties because sugar was in very short supply. During the War they were very scarce and strictly rationed. Even after the War they were hard to come by and were great treats for children. It was not until 1951 that sweets could be bought without ration tokens. These children are looking at a shop window full of sweets, something they had never seen before.

**Free milk** After many years of food shortages there was worry about the health of children who had been brought up on a poor war-time diet. In the Fifties the Government tried to make up for this deficiency by giving free milk at school every day. Very young children were given free orange juice, cod-liver oil and other healthy tonics which were full of body-building vitamins. Slowly the general health of the population improved.

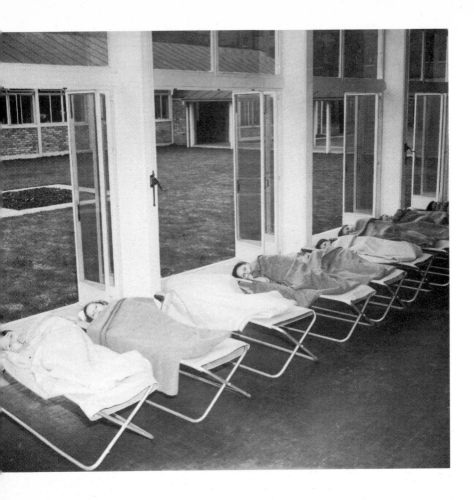

## Special health schools

Because of poor housing conditions and bad diets, children were sometimes delicate or suffered from diseases like tuberculosis. The new National Health Service (started in 1948) provided free medicine and health care for all, and it also provided special schools for delicate children. This school was built on a bomb-site in London's East End. Fresh air was very important to these children so they did their lessons and took rest periods in light, airy rooms and had gardens to play in. Schools like this were built in many parts of Britain.

**New schools** Besides free medical treatment, the Government also wanted to provide free education for everyone. New schools were built all over the country so that children could learn in modern, pleasant surroundings. The schools were provided with large playgrounds so that children no longer had to play on bomb sites. Schools like this, which were built in the Fifties, are still being used today.

## High-rise flats

To replace the bomb sites and slums new housing was built as quickly as possible. Flats were cheaper and quicker to erect than houses, so huge estates of high-rise flats were built. These became known as 'streets in the sky' and although people were happy to have clean, modern flats at first, they soon missed the friendliness of streets in which everyone knew and could help their neighbours. Some people were very unhappy in these flats and some of the children, who hadn't enough space to play in, started causing damage (they are called vandals). Today we realize that huge blocks of flats may not be the answer to the housing shortage problem.

**'Horror comics'** During and after the War there was a shortage of paper and so children's comics were quite rare. In the Fifties some comics came to Britain from America. They were very colourful with pictures of monsters and criminals. Parents became alarmed at these 'horror comics' because they thought they had a bad effect on children. They were pleased when *The Eagle* appeared, as it was educational as well as entertaining. The front page of *The Eagle* showed the adventurous Dan Dare, a space pilot who became a children's hero of the Fifties.

## The Festival of Britain

The war years and the ones that followed it had been grim and drab. As things slowly became brighter it was decided to hold a celebration to show people what a more prosperous future could hold. In 1951 the Festival of Britain was held in London. There was a huge funfair and many exhibitions showing Britain's progress in arts, architecture and science.

There was a Dome of Discovery showing the wonders of science, and the Skylon which was a thin, cigar-shaped tube towering above the exhibition ground. When lit at night, it looked like a glowing rocket. The Festival was a great success, visited by over 8 million people.

# The Coronation

Queen Elizabeth's father — King George VI — died in 1952. In June 1953 the Queen was crowned amid great splendour. It was the grandest occasion in the whole decade and thousands of people set out for London to watch the procession winding its way from Buckingham Palace to Westminster Abbey, and to wave as the Queen passed in her magnificent golden State Coach. About 30,000 London children had free seats to watch the procession but many more waited all night, and slept on the pavements with their parents, to catch a glimpse.

The whole ceremony was shown on television, which was a great luxury in those days. For many children it was the first time they had seen TV.

All over the country street parties were arranged, with long tables being set up and children celebrating with slap-up teas — just like the Jubilee in 1977, twenty-five years later. Millions of school children received commemorative mugs and other souvenirs of the great occasion.

**Mount Everest conquered** On the morning of the Coronation the news came through that Everest, the highest mountain in the world, had at last been climbed. This added to the excitement of the great day because the climbers were members of a Commonwealth team led by Sir John Hunt. The two men who reached the summit were Edmund Hillary, from New Zealand and Sherpa Tenzing, from the Himalayas. This picture, taken by Hillary, shows Tenzing holding the Union Jack aloft on the world's highest place.

# The Boys and Girls Exhibition A

popular annual event in the Fifties was the 'Boys and Girls Exhibition' at Olympia in London. In this huge hall were many interesting exhibits including trains, planes, bicycles and toys. In 1956 the theme was space travel, with futuristic spacecraft hanging from the roof. The exhibition was immensely popular with children in the Fifties.

**The Royal children** Two of the most famous children of the decade were Prince Charles and Princess Anne, the son and daughter of the Queen. There was great interest in the children

as they grew up. Here they are playing with
their toys at Balmoral Castle in Scotland in 1952,
when Prince Charles was nearly four and Princess
Anne two years old.

## Crazes of the Fifties

Here you can see girls spinning hula hoops by moving their hips as if they were Hawaiian hula dancers. This was thought to be great fun and very good for the figure! Boys were more interested in dressing like Davy Crockett whose adventures had been shown in a popular Walt Disney film, and they wore fur hats with 'tails' dangling down the back – like the raccoon skin headwear worn by Crockett.

**The 'affluent society'** Gradually the country and its people grew more affluent (richer) and started to catch up with the United States which was the world's richest nation. There, luxuries like cars, televisions and refrigerators, were considered quite normal. This picture shows a better-off home in Britain. Television was more common in homes by now but notice the tiny screen — a 14-inch set (35 cms) was large in those days! There is new furniture, the children are well dressed and even sweets are plentiful. The comic on the carpet is *Robin* which was the younger version of *Eagle*.

# 'Children's Hour'

Although more families were buying televisions, radio was still the most popular medium for entertainment. Most children listened to *Children's Hour* every day. The adventures of Larry the Lamb in *Toytown* were very popular. Later Larry (seen here with the grumpy Mr Growser) and his friends, transferred to television as a puppet series.

# Radio programmes

*The Goon Show* was one of the most popular of all radio comedy programmes. It starred Peter Sellers, Harry Secombe and Spike Milligan, playing such idiotic characters as Eccles, Bluebottle and Neddy Seagoon, and children drove their parents mad by imitating their voices.

In the Fifties the BBC broadcast on three radio channels — the Home Service, the Light Programme and the Third Programme. Pop music was discouraged and very little of it was heard except on Radio Luxembourg, a commercial radio station which could be heard in the evenings.

## Saturday morning 'flicks'

Before television became widespread, the cinema was nearly as popular as radio. This picture is from Walt Disney's film *Peter Pan*, one of the great successes of the time with children, along with *The Adventures Of Davy Crockett, Lady And The Tramp* and *20,000 Leagues Under The Sea*. On Saturday mornings cinemas showed special programmes for children featuring cowboy, space adventure and cartoon films. When most families owned a television the 'Saturday morning flicks' were discontinued and the cinema went into a decline. Many cinemas were turned into Bingo halls to cater for the gambling craze that was introduced from America.

# First generation television

The very popular programme *Blue Peter* was first shown on BBC TV in 1958. It was introduced by Leila Williams (who you can see here) and Christopher Trace. Until 1956, BBC was the only channel on television but in that year ITV broadcast for the first time and soon became very popular. So many people watched ITV that the BBC had to change its viewing hours. It used to stop broadcasting between 6.00 and 7.00 p.m. so that parents could get their children off to bed more easily. ITV carried on with its programmes through this hour so the BBC decided to do the same.

**Holiday camps** In the difficult days after the War, families could not afford to go away on holidays. Indeed, many children had never seen the sea! But as the country's finances improved and money became more readily available, families began taking holidays. Most people stayed in Britain — foreign travel did not become

popular until the Sixties – and millions went to specially built holiday camps where they could enjoy a great variety of activities. Butlins and Pontins were the most popular. They provided all sorts of amenities including chalets to stay in, swimming pools, sports, playgrounds and night-time entertainments.

# 'Latchkey kids'

As industry boomed there was plenty of work for everyone and for the first time millions of women started to take jobs. But this brought problems because with mother out at work, children came home to an empty house after school and had to fend for themselves. These

were called 'latchkey kids' because they kept the front door key on a string round their necks. Many people worried about these unsupervised youngsters and blamed the increase in crime and vandalism on children, roaming the streets, because there was no one to look after them at home.

**'You've never had it so good'** Some
people enjoyed the new prosperity in a very
extravagant way. Lord and Lady Docker were so
rich that they not only had a superb new Daimler,
they also had it plated in gold! It made a big hit at
the Motor Show but many disapproved and
thought it was showing off their wealth unneces-
sarily. A few years later, Prime Minister Harold
MacMillan told the people of Britain, 'You've never
had it so good' and even ordinary people were
better off than they had ever been before.

## The family car

One of the benefits of the new prosperity that 'The Affluent Society' (as the boom was called) brought was the family car. Millions of people who had never dreamed of owning their own cars were now able to afford a small saloon. The Morris Minor was solidly built, dependable and very popular. Later came the tiny 'Bubble Car'. The picture below shows a 1958 Messerschmitt Tiger – it carries the same name as the fighter aircraft that battled with Spitfires over Britain only a few years before.

**American limousines** Life was much easier in the United States where most people were very prosperous compared to people in war-torn Europe. The car industry was booming; many families had two cars and fanciful monsters with gleaming chrome trim and 'wings' sprouting at each end were very fashionable. Many young Britons dreamed of owning one of these limousines – but had to settle for something much more modest – perhaps a motor scooter which was just becoming popular.

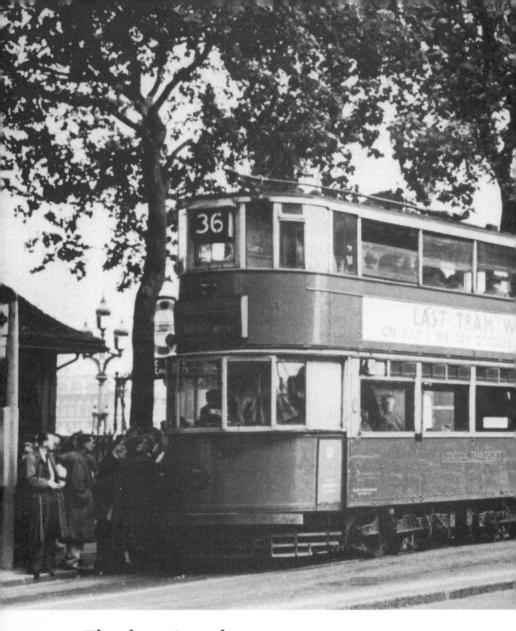

**The last London tram** Trams ran on rails
sunk into the road, which made them unsuitable
for the fast-moving traffic conditions of the Fifties.
In 1952, the last London trams ran through the
city. This one is making a final trip along the
Embankment, beside the Houses of Parliament.

Other old and familiar methods of transport were also gradually disappearing. The railways were being modernized and changing over from steam to electric and diesel engines. No longer would a puffing steam engine be seen on British Rail's tracks.

## The 'baby boom'

One form of transport was on the increase – the baby's pram! In Britain and the United States there was a 'baby boom' – more babies were born in these countries than at any other time in history. This was due to greater prosperity and because of better health care which meant that fewer babies and children died in their early years.

## 'Mini-adults'

Although people had more money to spend on clothes, children were not dressed in their own styles. Instead, they were given smaller versions of their parents' fashions. This was because children and teenagers were considered to be 'mini-adults'. It wasn't until teenagers discovered their own music – rock 'n' roll – that they started demanding their own styles. This picture shows 'look-alike' swimsuits for mother and daughter.

# Rock 'n' Roll

When rock 'n' roll burst into life in 1955, young people realized they had a type of music that was all their own, because their parents hated it. Soon they had their own dances such as the jive which they are doing here. They started making their own fashions – the men were Teddy Boys, so-called because of the Edwardian-style clothes they wore. Notice their slicked-back hair, the long 'drape' jackets, and the thick-soled shoes. Girls also wore their hair long, sometimes in a pony-tail. They liked dancing in blouses, very full skirts with billowing petticoats underneath which swirled out as they turned and wide belts, tight at the waist.

## Skiffle

**Skiffle** Teenagers not only had their own music, rock 'n' roll, they *made* their own music. This was Skiffle which originated in Traditional Jazz bands and was developed by Lonnie Donegan. Skiffle was easy to play, all you needed was a guitar, a washboard for rhythm, and a bass made out of a tea chest, a broom handle and some string. Thousands of young people started playing music for the first time and from these simple beginnings many pop stars were to find fame. In Liverpool there was a group called The Quarrymen and later two of its members — John Lennon and Paul McCartney — went on to form The Beatles.

**Smogs** Life still wasn't easy for people in the Fifties. In the big cities, chimneys belched foul smoke into the air because coal was the main form of heating. This caused terrible fogs, especially in London. The Great 'Smog' (smoky fog) of 1952 caused thousands of deaths, particularly

from bronchitis. This couple are groping their way home in masks that were supposed to protect them. Soon after the Clean Air Act was introduced, which allowed only smokeless fuels like coke to be burned, and the terrible smogs soon became a thing of the past.

**Immigrants** In the Fifties Britain was seen as a paradise for people living in countries that were part of the British Commonwealth. Poor conditions and unemployment in their countries, caused them to flock to Britain because they believed they could make a better life here. Many thousands came from the West Indies and Pakistan. By 1956 they were entering the country at a rate of about 3000 every month. Before long, there were too many immigrants for the homes and jobs available. It soon became a problem to find places for them to settle, especially as many British people resented them. The picture shows immigrants arriving at a London station.

**Race riots** Sometimes the resentment of British people led to violence. This racial prejudice, particularly among young whites who did not have jobs, reached an unpleasant peak in 1958 in the London district of Notting Hill, where gangs of young whites terrorized any black people they saw on the streets. This was the first example of continuing hostility.

## Schemes for the young

The violence among young people was growing. More crimes were committed by teenagers than ever before. This was believed to be caused by boredom in the young and so ways were sought to redirect their energies. These included youth clubs and the Outward Bound courses which gave youngsters a taste of adventure and taught them self-reliance. These boys are being taught rock-climbing on an Outward Bound Course.

The Duke of Edinburgh, the Queen's husband, was also concerned about the problems of young people. He founded the Duke of Edinburgh's Award Scheme in which teenagers could gain awards in many different pursuits.

**The 'four-minute mile'** One of the decade's heroes was Roger Bannister who clocked-up an historic athletic milestone when he became the first man ever to run a mile in less than four minutes. In 1954, with the help of other runners as pace-makers, he broke the record, having completed the mile in 3 minutes 59.4 seconds.

# 2 The Cold War

The mushroom shape of the cloud which arose following an atomic bomb explosion, seemed to loom over the whole decade.

In 1945 the United States brought an end to the war with Japan by dropping the atom bomb, the most terrifying weapon ever used, on the cities of Hiroshima and Nagasaki.

After the Second World War there followed what was known as 'The Cold War', between the countries of the West – notably America and Britain – and the Communist countries headed by Russia. This was a period of fear. The atom bomb was so hideously destructive that each side was terrified the other might use it first, and both sides raced to make bigger and more destructive bombs with the purpose of persuading – or deterring – the 'enemy' from going to war. Each side guarded its secrets jealously and employed secret agents to spy on the 'enemy'.

This fear resulted in a spate of 'spy scares', and many – perhaps innocent – people were convicted of passing secrets to the 'enemy'. The fear of atomic warfare and its consequences also induced a great revulsion in the minds of many people, who formed anti-nuclear movements in different parts of the world. This picture was taken over Nagasaki in Japan in 1945.

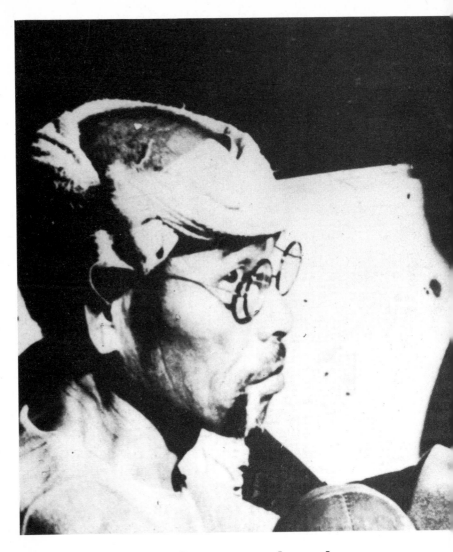

**The effects of the atom bomb** These are survivors of the bombing of Hiroshima. They show the terrible burns which resulted from the intense heat generated by the atomic explosion. Other long-term effects soon became evident and it was seen that the after effects of nuclear explosion could be even more terrible than those of the blast itself.

After the explosion came the terrible radioactive dust called fall-out, which caused awful sickness leading to death. The fall-out was feared to contaminate (poison) milk, water and food. As the race for bigger and more effective bombs developed, millions of people in Britain and other countries of the world became convinced that nuclear bombs should be banned.

## C.N.D. marches

In Britain the people who opposed the making and testing of atomic and nuclear bombs formed themselves into the Campaign for Nuclear Disarmament — C.N.D. They protested against further research into atomic science and held a huge march each year at Easter. Here

you see them in 1959 walking the 54 miles (87 km) from the atomic research establishment at Aldermaston in Berkshire to Trafalgar Square in London. Thousands of young people joined C.N.D. and wore its badge which was made up of the semaphore signals for N and D.

# The Russian leader

For a while Nikita Khrushchev, the Russian leader, was one of the most hated men in the world. The Americans feared the power of Russia's nuclear strength and were convinced that Khrushchev and other Russians were trying to spread Communism in the United States. Eventually, however, Khrushchev visited America and the two countries became less suspicious of each other. American and Russian leaders met regularly and tensions gradually decreased, although antagonism still continued between the world's two most powerful nations.

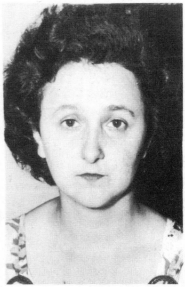

# Spy trials

There were many spy trials and spy scares during the Fifties, particularly in the United States, where Ethel and Julius Rosenberg were convicted of passing atomic secrets to the Russians. Concern about spying reached near-hysteria in America. The Rosenbergs were subsequently executed but many people today believe they may have been innocent.

**James Bond, 007** While the papers were full of stories about real-life and supposed spies, the most famous fictional spy was created. In 1953 Ian Fleming's book *Casino Royale* was published. This introduced the master spy James Bond, 007, to the world. 'James Bond' books became increasingly popular throughout the Fifties, reaching the cinema screen in the next decade. The picture shows Sean Connery as the master spy.

DF-13

## 'Witch hunts' in America
The threat of spies and Communist agents caused panic in the United States. Senator Joe McCarthy led a campaign to 'expose' all people suspected of being Communists. He conducted a series of 'trials' to discover Communist sympathizers, although he seldom bothered with evidence. People went in fear of McCarthy's 'witch hunts' because of the power he had to ruin their lives.

**War in Korea** In June 1950 troops from Communist North Korea invaded non-Communist South Korea and captured its capital, Seoul. The Second World War had only been over for five years, but troops from many nations, especially Britain and the United States, again found themselves fighting, in support of South Korea. People in the West were afraid of Communist attack in other countries which might result in another world war. The war in Korea lasted until 1953, during which time many were killed on both sides, and many more were made homeless.

# 3 The Years of Change

The Fifties was a decade of war, rebellion and revolution. The British Empire, which had stretched across the world, was breaking up. Peoples in the countries of the Empire wanted to rule themselves, and strove for independence from Britain. Many nations, particularly in Africa, tried to achieve this by violent means.

In Communist eastern Europe too, there was unrest. 1956 saw the Hungarian uprising against Russian repression, and in the Middle East, Egypt seized control of the Suez Canal.

The Civil Rights Movement in the United States was gathering momentum. Martin Luther King, the founder of the Movement, led many peace marches in order to try to gain equality for the black people of America.

But there were other, brighter, changes in the Fifties. The young had their own music and started making their own fashions. They had a new way of life — rock 'n' roll. The decade saw the birth of a new era when young people everywhere began to have a much larger say in how they wished to live and a much greater impact on the lives of those around them.

The picture shows Bill Haley and the Comets, the first rock 'n' roll band.

## Stars of rock 'n' roll

Rock 'n' roll was the first music that was entirely for and by young people and the first star was Bill Haley who had a huge hit with *Rock around the Clock*. But rock 'n' roll really took off when the young had a hero of their own age.

Elvis Presley was 21 when he burst into fame with *Heartbreak Hotel*. He had exactly the right sound for the times – hard, fast and sexy. He moved like a panther – his wriggling hips outraged adults and excited teenagers all over the world. He was nick-named 'Elvis the Pelvis'. His films were huge box office successes – here he is in *Jailhouse Rock* – and his records sold in millions. Elvis made rock 'n' roll *the* music of the young and started the rock and pop industry. After Elvis, young people were no longer simply 'mini-adults', they had their own cult with their own fashions, language, style and personalities.

Elvis had dozens of imitators in America and Britain. Among the most popular were Cliff Richard and Tommy Steele. Steele had his first hit in 1956 with *Rock with the Cave Man* and he also starred in films – here he is pictured making *Tommy the Toreador.*

Some rock 'n' roll stars were no older than their fans. Among them were Paul Anka who had a big hit, *Diana,* when he was only 15 and Brenda Lee (above) who first came to fame when she was 12! These teenage stars – who sang about things teenagers knew, proved that 'rock' and 'pop' were really the music of the young.

## The Hungarian uprising

In some parts of the world, young people had no time to enjoy rock 'n' roll. Some were not even allowed to hear it, particularly in Communist countries. There was great resentment in some of these countries against the lack of freedom. In Hungary in 1956 there was a revolt against the repression. The Russians put this down by the most brutal methods. Tanks rolled into the country and the Hungarians fought them with any weapons they could find. Children carried guns and blew up tanks with home-made petrol bombs. The fighting was terrible but eventually the well-armed Russians suppressed the rebellion. Thousands of Hungarians escaped from the Russians to the West and freedom.

# The Suez crisis

While the Hungarians were rebelling against the Russians, the Egyptians were taking over the Suez Canal. Britain had always been concerned about the Suez Canal because it was the shortest shipping route from the East to the West. The Canal had always been free to international shipping and without it ships had to make a long and expensive voyage around Africa. The British and French were outraged when the Egyptians took control of the Canal, and they sent troops to capture it in order to keep it open. The rest of the world did not support them in this and after some weeks of fighting, the British and French troops withdrew.

# World Refugee Year

This was a time of war and rebellion. The turmoil which resulted caused millions of people to become homeless refugees, fleeing to other countries in search of safety. The problem was so bad that 1959 was declared World Refugee Year in order to publicize their plight and give financial help. The children pictured here have had to make their homes in the shelter of a junk yard. The United Nations, who organized World Refugee Year, tried to ensure that these and other children could be housed in better conditions.

## Civil rights in America
In the United States black people were demanding to be treated equally with white people. In the Southern States black people were not allowed to eat in the same restaurants as white people, to sit next to them on buses, or to go to the same schools as white children.

In 1955 the United States' government declared that black and white children should be allowed to go to the same schools in seventeen Southern states. The authorities in those states did all they could to stop this. Here you can see two black boys being turned away from the high school in Little Rock, Arkansas, by jeering white students. Although the law was on the boys' side, the white students, often supported by police, and even soldiers, refused to let them in.

## Great men of the Fifties
Amid all this distress some great men emerged to lead their people and give cause for hope. Martin Luther King was a preacher who led the black struggle for Civil Rights. He advocated peaceful resistance and led many marches in protest against the laws that stopped black people in the United States from being treated equally with whites. Although he

met with violent opposition, his crusade was successful. Tragically, he was assassinated in 1968.

Pope John XXIII was a greatly loved pope. His gentleness, humanity and humility endeared him to people all over the world. He worked and prayed for peace, inspiring others with his sincerity and showing many that the world need not be torn by war and strife.

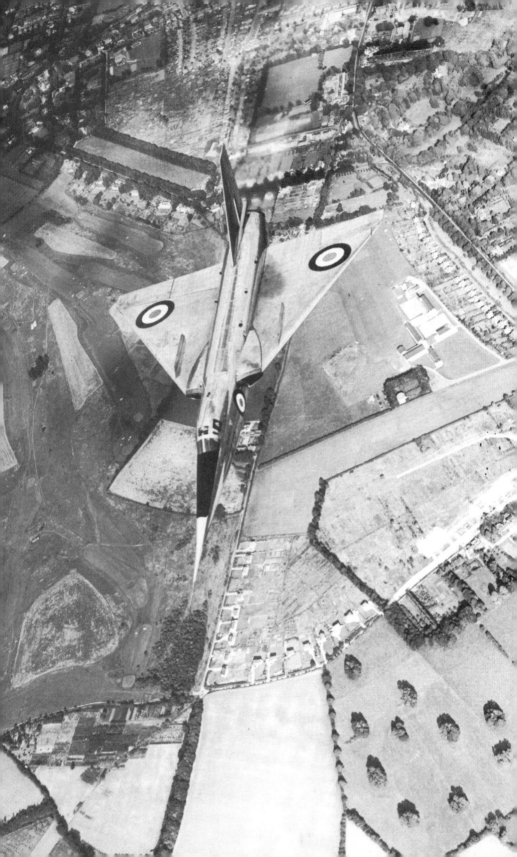

# 4  Science Fact and Science Fiction

The decade was a period of great scientific advance and there were many 'break-throughs' in medicine and technology. At last a vaccine was discovered which would immunize against the maiming disease – polio. Antibiotics were developed which almost stamped out tuberculosis – for centuries a killer disease.

The enormous store of energy released by the splitting of the atom, was at last harnessed to produce nuclear power which would provide fuel for future generations.

New jet planes could fly at speeds never before attained. Here is the Fairey Delta in which Peter Twiss set a new airspeed record of 1132 m.p.h. in 1956.

The decade also saw the dawning of the Space Age. In 1957 the Russians launched the first satellite, called Sputnik, and before the end of the Fifties they had sent spacecraft out to the far side of the moon.

Films and books of the time reflected everyone's absorbing interest in science and space. The 1950s saw the first of many sightings of UFOs (Unidentified Flying Objects). Science fact or science fiction? Or just fakes? We still don't know.

# A medical break-through

Science helped prevent one serious illness which particularly affected children – polio. This could cause paralysis in young people or even, in extreme

cases, death. But in the mid-Fifties a vaccine was developed to give protection against polio. Here you can see mothers and children queueing up for some of the first injections given in Britain.

**The Comet** The development of the jet engine meant that planes could fly at very high speeds. The Comet, pictured here, was the world's first jet airliner, and it led the way for the 'Jumbos' of today. Sadly, it was the first plane in which metal fatigue (the deterioration of metal caused by stress and strain) was found after a crash.

## The flying bedstead

Perhaps the most extraordinary flying machine of all was the 'flying bedstead'. This remarkable contraption was an early experiment in vertical take-off and landing. It may have looked crazy, but it contributed to the development of the Harrier 'jump jet' many years later.

## Overland to the South Pole 1957 was
declared International Geophysical Year when
scientists from many countries co-operated in
studying Earth. The most important areas of
research were into the oceans, weather, space and
exploration of the Antarctic.

The South Pole was explored by a Commonwealth Transantarctic Expedition. The British group, led by Vivian Fuchs, was the first to cross the Antarctic overland during a long journey in 1957 and 1958. He and his team reached the South Pole on January 20th, 1957 and completed the trek on March 2nd. When the expedition returned to Britain, Vivian Fuchs was knighted and these medals were struck in honour of his achievement.

# Nuclear power for electricity

Despite the Campaign for Nuclear Disarmament, not all atomic research was for warlike purposes. In 1956 Calder Hall, the world's first large-scale nuclear power station, was opened at Windscale in Cumberland. This generated electricity by nuclear

power instead of by burning solid fuels. The Americans launched a nuclear-powered submarine, the U.S.S. *Nautilus*, which was the first vessel ever to pass under the polar ice-cap. The Russians also launched a nuclear-powered ice-breaker which they named *Lenin*.

**Flying on the sea!** Entirely new forms of propulsion were being developed. Many people laughed at the idea of being carried over land and sea on a cushion of air, but Sir Christopher Cockerell proved his idea could work by developing the hovercraft. The forerunner of these modern machines first crossed the English Channel in July 1959. Today the hovercraft is accepted as a speedy way to carry people and cars across short stretches of water.

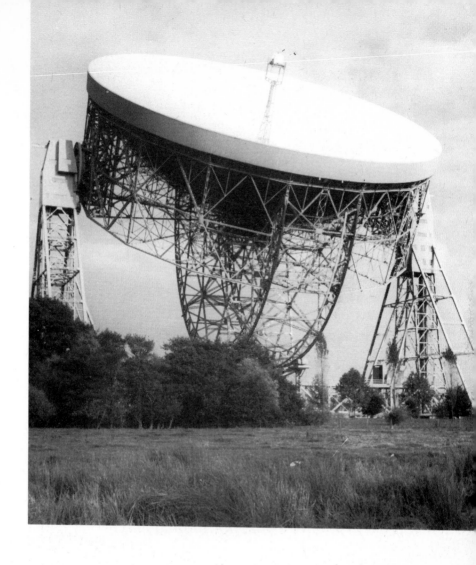

## The Jodrell Bank telescope

Eyes were turning to the heavens as the exploration of space at last seemed possible. Also following the stars was the Jodrell Bank radio telescope. It was opened in 1957. At one point money to complete the building of the telescope was so short that children started to collect funds towards its construction. It was this telescope that tracked the distinctive 'bleep-bleeps' of Sputnik (see page 90).

(see page 90)

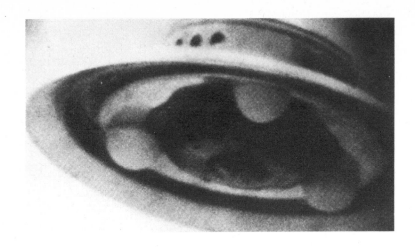

## 'UFOs'
Many people in the Fifties talked of 'flying saucers' – strange machines from other planets, and they claimed to have seen them. Here is a photograph of one taken by G. Adamski in California, in 1952. He claimed it was about 10 metres across and about 6 metres deep, with underhanging globes that he believed were used to direct the craft.

This and other photographs caused great excitement throughout the decade. The United States started a study of reported sightings, most of which they said were weather balloons or other man-made machines. They didn't like the unscientific term 'flying saucers', so they called them Unidentified Flying Objects – UFOs.

## 'Sci-Fi' on the screen
The cinema reflected the interest in science fiction by making some highly imaginative films. Some were about Man going into the race to get into space, others about the possibilities of space creatures landing on earth. This scene is from *The Creature from the Black Lagoon*, a film about monsters. These were

often freak creatures which had grown in the wake of an atomic explosion, reflecting the concern people felt about the horrific possibilities of unleashing atomic power.

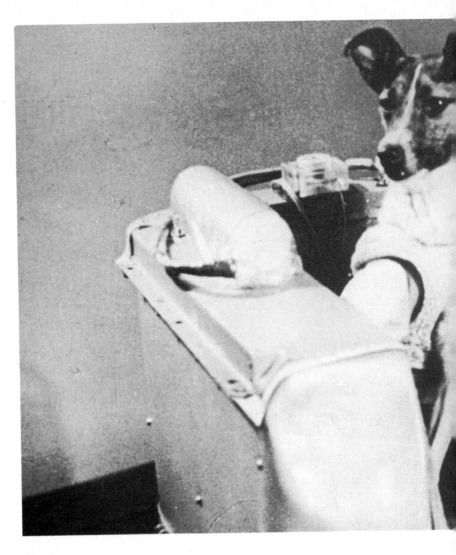

**Into space** Real space adventure happened in 1957 when the Russians launched satellites called sputniks into space. They orbited the earth and proved that the dream of launching men beyond earth's atmosphere was becoming a reality. Various animals – dogs and monkeys – were tested in these craft but manned flight was still a few years away. This dog, Laika, went into space in the second sputnik. In 1959 the Russians sent other craft,

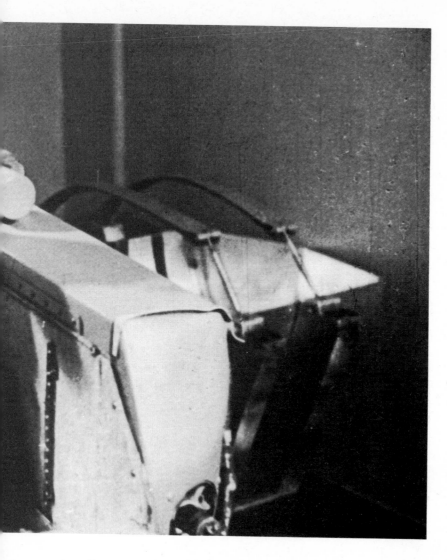

Luniks, around the moon to photograph its far side which had never been seen.

The United States had also attempted a space satellite launch in 1957 but it failed. The success of the Russians spurred the Americans into new efforts and the Space Race began, which culminated in the next decade with Neil Armstrong stepping onto the moon. The space age had dawned.

# New Words

| | |
|---|---|
| *antibiotics* | Chemical substances used by doctors to stop the growth of harmful germs. |
| *Civil Rights Movement* | A peaceful movement founded by Martin Luther King to try to gain equality for the black people of the United States, along with the white people. |
| *decade* | A series of ten years, e.g. 1950 to 1959. |
| *Edwardian* | An adjective to describe fashions worn during the reign of King Edward VII, early in the twentieth century. |
| *fall-out* | Radioactive dust from a nuclear explosion. |
| *limousine* | A large motor car. |
| *Lunik* | The name given to the Russian spacecraft which photographed the far side of the moon, in the late 1950s. |
| *medium* | Something through which communication is made, e.g. the press, the radio or the television. |
| *nuclear energy* | The atomic energy released by splitting atoms (notably of uranium and plutonium). |
| *pre-fab* | Abbreviation for pre-fabricated houses, which were quickly built from asbestos sheets in order to |

|            | provide homes for people made homeless by the War. |
|------------|----------------------------------------------------|
| *ration*   | A fixed amount of food or other commodities. Rationing was introduced in Britain during the War, when food and other items were in short supply, and continued for several years after the War, until supplies improved. |
| *Skylon*   | A tube which was shaped like a cigar, erected at the Festival of Britain in 1951. |
| *Sputnik*  | The first (Russian made) earth satellite. |
| *UFOs*     | Abbreviation for Unidentified Flying Objects, such as flying saucers. |
| *vaccine*  | A substance which is injected in order to prevent disease. |
| *vandals*  | People who carelessly or deliberately destroy buildings or works of art. |
| *Witch hunt* | The name given to Senator McCarthy's investigations of supposed Communists in the United States. |

# More Books

*A Short History of the Post-War World 1945– 1970* Duncan Taylor (Dobson)
*Casino Royale* Ian Fleming (Jonathan Cape)
*Growing up in World War II* Kathleen Monham (Wayland)
*Spies and Spying* David Sweetman (Wayland)
*The Forties and Fifties, an Illustrated History* Nathaniel Harris (MacDonald Educational)
*The Fifties* Peter Lewis (Heinemann)

## Picture acknowledgements

The author and publishers would like to thank all those who have given permission for copyright pictures to be reproduced on the following pages: American History Picture Library, 63, 64; Associated Press, 73; Atomic Energy Authority, 84–5; BBC Stills Library, 30, 31, 32; Catholic Herald, 75; Dezo Hoffman, 69; Flight International, 76; Radio Times Hulton Picture Library, *cover*, 6, 8, 11, 12, 13, 14, 15, 18, 21 *lower*, 23, 25, 26–7, 29, 44, 48–9, 50, 70, 75–9; London Features International, 66, 69; London Transport, 42–3; National Film Archives, United Artists, 62, M.G.M., 68, Universal, 89; National Motor Museum, 38, 39, 40; Novosti, 60, 90–91; Outward Bound Trust, 52; Paul Clark, 19; Popperfoto, 61, 71; Royal Geographical Society, 24, 82, 83; Miss Singleton, 47; Syndication International, 45; John Topham, *Frontispiece*, 20–21, 22; United Nations, 72; University of Manchester, 87; Walt Disney Productions, 33. All other pictures are from the Wayland Picture Library.

# Index